for beginners

Advanced SQL for Beginners

Master Complex Queries, Joins, Subqueries, and Stored Procedures for Database Management

Printed in the United States of America

First Edition: 2025

This copyright page includes the necessary copyright notice, permissions request information, acknowledgments for the cover design, interior design, and editing, as well as the details of the first edition.

www.littlebiggiant.com

Introduction

The room smelled faintly of burnt coffee. A monitor glowed. Rows of numbers blurred into red errors. A student named Sam stared at the screen. Fingers hovered over the keyboard. The query had run for seconds and then everything changed. Orders vanished from the table. The dashboard showed negative sales. "What did that query just do?" came out small and sharp. The face in the monitor looked older. Fear tightened the throat. Close-up, the code seemed like a locked door. Behind that door were joins, subqueries, and stored procedures—tools that sounded powerful and scary at the same time. SQL has been the standard language for relational databases since ANSI adopted it in 1986. That fact mattered now because businesses still use those same rules. The wrong join can hide a customer. A missing WHERE can delete a month of work. The book Advanced SQL for Beginners promises to teach those exact things: how to build complex queries, use joins correctly, write safe subqueries, and run stored procedures that do jobs inside the database. The promise felt urgent at two in the morning.

Hands shook. Sam opened the chapter called Master Complex Queries, Joins, Subqueries, and Stored Procedures for Database Management. The first example showed a simple join that matched customers to orders. The example worked, clear as a bell. It fixed one row. But there were hundreds more. "This is impossible," Sam thought. The mind jumped between panic and a stubborn kind of curiosity. If one short, correct query could pull the missing data back where it belonged, then learning the right steps mattered more than ever. If it could not, then a real problem loomed for a real company relying on those numbers. Which route would the next query take—repair or ruin—and who would find the single clean line of SQL that made everything right?

Table of Contents

Table of Contents **7**
Chapter 1 .... **10**
Foundations of Advanced SQL 10
Chapter 2 .... **30**
Mastering Joins and Set Operators 30
Chapter 3 .... **53**
Window Functions and Analytical Querying 53
Chapter 4 .... **69**
Subqueries, CTEs and Derived Tables 69
Chapter 5 .... **89**
Advanced Aggregation and Grouping Techniques 89
Chapter 6 .... **109**
Query Optimization and Indexing 109
Chapter 7 .... **130**
Transactions, Concurrency and Reliability 130
Chapter 8 .... **148**
Stored Procedures, Functions and Triggers 148
Chapter 9 .... **172**
Security, Auditing and Defensive SQL 172
Chapter 10 .... **191**

Real-World Patterns, Migration and Monitoring... 191

Chapter 1

Foundations of Advanced SQL

By the end of this chapter, you will understand the foundations that support advanced SQL: how keys, normalization, and data types shape clean databases; how SQL dialects differ and why portability matters; and how to build a repeatable, reliable workflow for writing, testing, and version-controlling your queries.

Foundations: Relational model essentials—keys, normalization, and data typing

1) Identify keys and relationships. Keys are the anchors that keep data connected and consistent. A primary key is a unique identifier for each row in a table. A candidate key is any field (or combination of fields) that could serve as a unique identifier. A foreign key is a field (or set of fields) that links one table to another, establishing a relationship between records. When you design a database, you start by deciding what will be the primary key for each table and how tables will relate to each other through foreign keys. Think of a school system: a Students table might use StudentID as its primary key, and an Enrollments table might use

EnrollmentID as its primary key while including a StudentID that points back to the Students table. This simple link creates a relationship: each enrollment belongs to one student, and you can walk from a student to every course they've enrolled in, or from a course to every student who has enrolled. The key idea is to keep each fact in a single place and use keys to connect related facts without duplicating them.

2) Normalize data to reduce redundancy. Normalization is a design habit that helps keep the data tidy and easy to update. In practical terms, it means putting related information into separate, logically linked tables so you don't repeat the same data over and over. The goal isn't to make

everything complicated; it's to prevent odd things from happening when you change or delete data. For example, if you kept a student's name, birthdate, and contact details in the same big table as their course enrollments, updating an address or correcting a misspelled name would require changing many rows. By splitting information into a Students table and an Enrollments table, you update the address once in Students and let Enrollments reference that student through the StudentID key. Normalization helps your database stay accurate as it grows, and it makes queries faster and more predictable because you're always pulling data from the right place.

3) Choose data types and enforce constraints. The data type you pick for each column matters more than you might think. A date field should be stored with a date type, not as a string, so you can easily sort by date, compute ages, and compare dates. Numbers should use numeric types so arithmetic and totals are precise. Text fields need sensible length limits to prevent wasted space and to catch mistakes (for example, a phone number field should be long enough for country codes but not endless). Constraints are the guardrails that keep data honest. NOT NULL demands a value; UNIQUE ensures no two rows share a value in a column when that's not allowed; CHECK can enforce simple rules (like a grade between A and F). If you set up a Students table with StudentID as the primary key, a NOT NULL name field, and a

birthdate with a valid date type, you're building a solid foundation that supports accurate queries and trustworthy results. A small, concrete example helps bring this to life: in a simplified system, you might store StudentID as an integer, name as a short text string, and BirthDate as a date. In Enrollments, you'd store EnrollmentID as a unique key, StudentID as a foreign key referencing Students, and CourseCode as a short text. The elegance of the design shows up in the way you can join these tables confidently, knowing the links are sound.

Example 1 (micro-case): A simple student-and-enrollment design. You create a Students table with StudentID (PK), Name, and

BirthDate. You create an Enrollments table with EnrollmentID (PK), StudentID (FK), CourseCode, and EnrollmentDate. Because Students and Enrollments are linked by StudentID, you can answer questions like "Which courses is this student enrolled in?" without duplicating student data in every enrollment row. If a student's name changes, you update it once in Students; if a course code changes, you update it in the Courses reference (not in every enrollment row). This is normalization in action.

Example 2 (micro-case): Keeping contact information tidy. Suppose you start with a big table that mixes students, teachers, and staff in one messy sheet. The normalization habit suggests splitting into separate People and Roles tables, with a PeopleID as the shared key and a Roles table that describes what each person does. The result is clearer data and fewer places to fix when a phone number changes or a person switches roles. You're not inventing new concepts here; you're applying well-known principles to keep data coherent as the system grows.

Key takeaways from this section: design around stable keys; separate concerns so related facts live in dedicated places; and enforce sensible data types and constraints to protect accuracy. When you plan with these ideas, you'll be better prepared to work across any SQL environment and to ask the right questions about data quality.

Coming up next: Mastering dialect differences, portability, and vendor-specific features. In the next section, you'll learn how SQL is standardized but reality varies by database, and you'll pick practical strategies to keep your queries reliable across systems.

Foundations: Relational model essentials—continuation through Section 2

4) SQL dialect differences and portability. SQL is a common language, but databases speak with slightly different accents. Some differences show up in tiny details like how you quote identifiers (using

double quotes in some systems, backticks in others), how you concatenate strings (some use CONCAT, others use the || operator), or how you request a limited number of rows (LIMIT in some systems, FETCH FIRST in others). There are also differences in supported data types and in how functions behave. When you write a query, you can rely on the core rules of SQL, but you should expect small tweaks if you run the same query on a different database. The practical approach is to write core queries in standard SQL when possible, and isolate any vendor-specific features in separate modules so you can swap them out without changing the whole codebase.

5) Portability and vendor-specific features. Portability means your code can run on multiple database systems with minimal changes. To stay portable, favor standard SQL and avoid nonessential vendor tricks in your core queries. When you must use vendor-specific features to get a big win in performance or capability, isolate those features in views, stored procedures, or adapter layers so the rest of your codebase remains stable. For example, if you rely on a database's advanced window function capabilities, keep that logic in a module that can be swapped if you move to a different system. This habit makes future migrations or cloud moves less painful and helps teams stay productive even when the tech stack shifts.

6) Vendor-specific features and caveats. Some features exist across many databases, but their details differ. Window functions, for instance, appear in most modern systems, but you'll still run into syntax or behavior differences in edge cases. Date and time handling, JSON storage, and certain optimizer hints also vary. The safe rule is to know what your target database supports and to test critical queries in that environment. When you're learning, it's okay to explore a feature in one system, but document how it would translate elsewhere and be ready to adjust if you change engines. The payoff is not about mastering every nuance at once but about learning to think in

portable terms and to flag where cross-database compatibility matters.

Example 2 (micro-case): A portability test. You write a query to list customers and their order totals. In PostgreSQL, you might rely on standard aggregation, but in another system you discover a slight difference in date arithmetic or string handling when joining orders to customers. You design the query in a way that uses straightforward joins, standard grouping, and explicit column names, then you test it on the systems you care about. If you must adapt for a specific vendor, you wrap the vendor-specific bits in a small, isolated module so the rest of your code remains stable.

Development workflows: writing, testing, and version-controlling queries

7) Start with a plan and write incrementally. Before you type a single line of SQL, outline what you want to learn or prove: which tables you'll read, what joins you'll perform, and what the final result should look like. Then write a simple version of the query and test it. Add one feature at a time—filters, sorts, computed columns—so you can see how each change affects the result. The rationale is simple: small, verifiable steps make debugging much faster and give you clear feedback about what works and what doesn't.

8) Version control and reproducible environments. Put your query files into a folder that resembles a tiny project: a readme, a data blueprint, and a few query files with clear names. Use a version-control system to save changes with meaningful messages like "add customer join" or "switch to standard SQL." Keep a seed dataset or a small sample database that reproduces the same results every time you run the queries. The benefit is reliability: you can roll back to a known state, share exact queries with teammates, and track how your thinking evolves.

9) Testing, debugging, and refactoring. Treat queries like code: test them, fix errors, and refactor for clarity. Use simple checks to verify results—for

example, count rows, verify that sums match expectations, or compare results across related tables. If a query runs slowly, ask why by looking at the plan or by testing with smaller data slices. Refactor by breaking complex queries into smaller parts: common table expressions (CTEs) or temporary views can make the logic easier to read and maintain. The aim is a dependable, readable workflow that you can repeat when new data arrives or when requirements change.

Two brief examples of the workflow in action

Example A (micro-case): You're asked to generate a quarterly report of enrollments by course. You start by outlining the tables (Students, Enrollments, Courses) and the fields you need (course name, count of enrollments, quarter). You write a simple query to count enrollments per course for the quarter, run it on a seed dataset, and check that the numbers look reasonable. You then add a date filter, confirm the results again, and finally refactor using a small CTE to keep the logic clean. The outcome is a clear, repeatable pattern you can reuse for future quarters.

Example B (micro-case): You need a portable query to list customers who placed orders in the last 30 days. You write standard SQL that uses explicit joins and clear time arithmetic. You run it on your current database, then test on another system you plan to support. If you encounter a dialect mismatch, you move the vendor-specific bit to a separate layer and keep the rest portable. The result is a robust query set that travels with you, not a fragile cliff you fall off when you switch engines.

Key takeaways from this chapter: foundations matter more than flash. A stable relational model with thoughtful keys, disciplined normalization, and well-chosen data types makes data trustworthy and queries reliable. Understanding dialect differences helps you write code that's easier to port, and a clear development workflow—from planning to version control to testing—keeps your work repeatable and scalable. With these habits, you're ready to tackle the next layer of SQL power, starting with the practical art of joins and set operations.

Coming up next: Mastering Joins and Set Operators. In Chapter 2 you'll learn how to connect data across tables with inner, left, right, and full joins; explore self-joins, semi-joins, and anti-joins for more complex relationships; and master the key set operators—UNION, INTERSECT, and EXCEPT—to reason about results in new ways. Subtittle: Mastering Joins and Set Operators

Chapter 2

Mastering Joins and Set Operators

By the end of this chapter, you will master inner, left, right, and full outer joins, along with self-joins, semi-joins, and anti-joins, plus the set operators UNION, INTERSECT, and EXCEPT, including how to order results and how duplicates are handled in each case.

Inner, Left, Right, and Full Outer Joins in Real-World Models

A join is how you connect two tables so you can see related data together. The most common is the inner join. It returns only the rows where the keys match in both tables. Think of two lists: customers and orders. If you join them on customer_id, you see every customer who has placed at least one order, along with their order details. If a customer never placed an order, they won't appear in an inner join result.

Example 1: Inner join between customers and orders

```
SELECT c.customer_id, c.name, o.order_id,
o.total
FROM customers AS c
JOIN orders AS o ON c.customer_id =
o.customer_id;
```

Explanation: This shows each customer who has at least one order, with the matching order information. If you want to see customers who placed multiple orders, you'll see multiple rows for that customer—one per order.

A left outer join gives you all rows from the left table (the first one you mention) and the matching rows from the right table. If there's no match, you still keep the left row, but the right-side columns become NULL. This is useful when you want to know who exists in the primary list but might not have related records elsewhere.

Example 2: Left join customers to orders

SELECT c.customer_id, c.name, o.order_id, o.total

FROM customers AS c

LEFT JOIN orders AS o ON c.customer_id = o.customer_id

ORDER BY c.customer_id;

Explanation: You'll see every customer. For customers without orders, o.order_id and o.total will be NULL. This helps you identify customers who may need attention, like marketing outreach or order follow-ups.

A right outer join is the mirror image: all rows from the right table appear, with matching rows from the left, and NULLs where there's no match. It's less common than left joins but powerful when the right table holds the primary reference data you care about.

Example 3: Right join (customers on the left, orders on the right)

```
SELECT c.customer_id, c.name, o.order_id,
o.total
FROM customers AS c
RIGHT JOIN orders AS o ON c.customer_id =
o.customer_id
ORDER BY o.order_id;
```

Explanation: You'll see all orders, including any that were created by customers not listed in the customers table (if such data exists in your schema). In practice, many systems avoid this scenario, but the right join is useful when the "many side" may include records without corresponding entries on the "one side."

Full outer joins combine both left and right joins. They return all rows from both tables, matching where possible, and filling with NULLs where there is no match. Not all databases support full outer joins, so check your vendor's capabilities. When you can use them, they're ideal for reconciling data from two sources that you expect to be largely aligned but not perfectly.

Example 4: Full outer join

SELECT a.id AS a_id, a.value AS a_value, b.id AS b_id, b.value AS b_value

FROM table_a AS a

```
FULL OUTER JOIN table_b AS b ON a.id = b.id
ORDER BY COALESCE(a.id, b.id);
```

Explanation: You see every row from both sides. If a row exists only in A, b_id and b_value will be NULL; if it exists only in B, a_id and a_value will be NULL. Full outer joins help you see gaps and overlaps in two datasets side by side.

What to watch for:

- Joins can dramatically change row counts. Inner joins typically shrink results; outer joins can expand them.

- NULLs appear in non-matching sides of outer joins. You'll often need to filter or handle NULLs in downstream logic.

- When working with large datasets, consider the join order and indexing. Joins on well-indexed keys run faster, and sometimes rewriting to subqueries or derived tables helps performance.

Self-Joins, Semi-Joins, and Anti-Joins for Complex Relationships

A self-join is when you join a table to itself. This is perfect for hierarchical data or two records that share a relationship within the same dataset. You can see this in organizations, where you want to connect each employee to their manager.

Example 1: Self-join to show employee and manager names

```
SELECT e.employee_id, e.name AS
employee_name, m.name AS manager_name
FROM employees AS e
LEFT JOIN employees AS m ON e.manager_id =
m.employee_id
ORDER BY e.employee_id;
```

Explanation: Every employee is listed with their manager's name when available. If an employee has no manager listed, manager_name will be NULL. This is useful for org charts, mentorship programs, or reporting structures.

A semi-join returns rows from the first table if a related row exists in the second table. It answers questions like: "Which customers have placed at least one order?" Semi-joins keep the columns from the first table only, but use the second table to filter.

Example 2: Semi-join using EXISTS

SELECT c.customer_id, c.name

```
FROM customers AS c
WHERE EXISTS (
  SELECT 1
  FROM orders AS o
  WHERE o.customer_id = c.customer_id
);
```

Explanation: You get every customer who has at least one order. The result does not include any order data, just the customer data that has a match.

An anti-join returns rows from the first table where there is no related row in the second table.

This is useful for spotting gaps, such as customers who have not placed any orders yet.

Example 3: Anti-join with NOT EXISTS

```
SELECT c.customer_id, c.name
FROM customers AS c
WHERE NOT EXISTS (
  SELECT 1
  FROM orders AS o
  WHERE o.customer_id = c.customer_id
);
```

Explanation: You see customers who have no orders. This helps with targeted outreach, onboarding strategies, or data-cleaning tasks where you want to identify incomplete records.

Putting self-joins, semi-joins, and anti-joins together, you can model complex relationships inside a single dataset. Self-joins reveal chains of relationships; semi-joins confirm presence of related data; anti-joins reveal absence. Together, they give you a sharper view of how data connects, where it's missing, and how to act on those findings.

Set Operators: UNION, INTERSECT, and EXCEPT

Set operators combine the results of two queries into a single result. They're powerful for comparing datasets, consolidating lists, and removing or preserving duplicates as needed. The big ideas to remember are how they handle duplicates and how results are ordered.

Example 1: UNION versus UNION ALL

```
SELECT country FROM customers

UNION

SELECT country FROM suppliers
```

```
ORDER BY country;
```

Explanation: UNION merges the two lists and removes duplicates. You'll get a clean, deduplicated list of countries that appear in either table.

If you want to keep duplicates (for example, if a country appears in both lists as separate records and you care about that repetition), use UNION ALL:

```
SELECT country FROM customers

UNION ALL
```

```
SELECT country FROM suppliers
ORDER BY country;
```

Explanation: UNION ALL keeps every occurrence, so a country that appears in both tables will show up twice in the final list.

Example 2: INTERSECT

```
SELECT country FROM customers
INTERSECT
SELECT country FROM suppliers
ORDER BY country;
```

Explanation: INTERSECT returns only the rows that appear in both results. You'll see countries that are present in both customers and suppliers datasets.

Note: Some databases require careful alignment of column names and types for set operators. The queries above assume the same single column with compatible types on both sides.

Example 3: EXCEPT (or MINUS in some systems)

SELECT country FROM customers

EXCEPT

SELECT country FROM suppliers

```
ORDER BY country;
```

Explanation: EXCEPT yields rows that are in the first result (customers) but not in the second (suppliers). It's handy for identifying items unique to one list. In systems that use MINUS instead of EXCEPT, the meaning is the same, but the keyword changes.

Semantics, Ordering, and Duplicate Handling

- UNION vs UNION ALL: UNION removes duplicates; UNION ALL keeps duplicates. Use UNION when you want a clean, non-redundant list.

Use UNION ALL when duplicates carry meaning or you're combining large results where you know duplicates exist and performance matters.

- INTERSECT: Returns distinct rows common to both sets. If you need to preserve duplicates, you'll typically need a different approach, because INTERSECT's standard behavior is to produce distinct results.

- EXCEPT (or MINUS): Returns rows from the first query that aren't in the second. Like INTERSECT, the default behavior emphasizes distinct results, not duplicates, so plan accordingly if duplicates matter in your use case.

- Ordering: For all set operators, you typically place ORDER BY at the very end of the combined result. Ordering inside subqueries generally doesn't affect the final order and can be ignored by the optimizer in many situations, though some databases allow ORDER BY in subqueries in specific contexts.

- Performance: Set operators can be expensive on large datasets. When possible, aim to push filtering down early in each subquery (WHERE clauses) and ensure columns used for joins and set operations are properly indexed. You can often rewrite complex logic as joins or as materialized intermediates to improve readability and speed.

Key Takeaway: Joins connect data across tables, while set operators combine and compare whole query results; mastering both gives you the power to build precise, readable data stories and to spot gaps, overlaps, and opportunities at a glance.

Coming up next Subtittle: Window Functions and Analytical Querying

1) Ranking and windowed aggregate functions for partitioned analysis,

2) Frame clauses, sliding windows and moving-average patterns,

3) Event sequencing, gaps-and-islands and sessionization techniques

Chapter 3

Window Functions and Analytical Querying

You will learn to use window functions to rank data within groups, apply frame clauses for moving averages, and sequence events into meaningful activity patterns—all with practical, beginner-friendly steps.

Ranking and windowed aggregate functions for partitioned analysis

Step 1: Decide what to partition by. The first move is to choose the group you want to compare inside. If you want each class or department to have its own ranking, you partition by that category. This keeps analyses fair and local. For example, you might rank students by score within each class, or rank sales by region within each month.

Step 2: Choose a window function that fits the goal. If you need a strict order with a unique number for every row, use ROW_NUMBER. If you want to treat ties the same way and leave gaps in the ranking, use RANK. If you want a ranking that assigns consecutive numbers to ties (no gaps), use DENSE_RANK. For a quick quartile-like split, NTILE can be handy.

Step 3: Tell SQL how to walk the window. You'll write OVER with PARTITION BY and ORDER BY to sculpt the window. The ORDER BY determines who sits above whom; the PARTITION BY keeps groups separate. For instance, to find the top student in each class, order by score descending and partition by class.

Step 4: See it in action with a simple class ranking. Consider a list of students with class IDs and scores. A query might look like this: ROW_NUMBER() OVER (PARTITION BY class_id ORDER BY score DESC) AS rank_in_class. This assigns 1 to the highest scorer in each class and counts downward within that class.

Step 5: Compare ranking behaviors. Test RANK and DENSE_RANK on the same data to see differences. If two students tie for the top score, RANK will assign 1 and 1 but leave a gap (2nd place is skipped), while DENSE_RANK will give 1 and 1 and continue with 2 for the next distinct score. This matters when you present standings or create tiered buckets.

Step 6: Build micro-cases to practice. Micro-case A: Rank students by score in their class, then show each student's rank and score. Micro-case B: Rank products by sales within each category, and expose how ties are handled. In both cases, observe how the chosen function shapes the result and what that means for reporting.

Two illustrative micro-cases you can try now help you see the difference clearly. Micro-case A might show that in Class A, three students share the top score; ROW_NUMBER would still give each a distinct rank, while RANK would show identical top ranks and skip the next number. Micro-case B could reveal that two products tie for second place in a category; DENSE_RANK would flood those ties with consecutive numbers, whereas RANK might leave a gap.

Frame clauses, sliding windows and moving-average patterns

Step 1: Pick the right window size. Frame clauses let you decide how many past and future rows to include around the current row. For moving averages, a common choice is a fixed-size sliding window like 7 days or 7 entries. For rolling sums or running totals, you can use an unbounded frame to accumulate as you go.

Step 2: Decide ROWS or RANGE semantics. ROWS is simpler and counts rows, so ROWS BETWEEN 6 PRECEDING AND CURRENT ROW gives you the last seven rows no matter what. RANGE uses the values in ORDER BY, which can behave differently with gaps in dates or nonuniform steps. In practice, ROWS is predictable for moving averages; RANGE can be tricky when the order has gaps.

Step 3: Implement a 7-day moving average. A standard pattern is AVG(value) OVER (ORDER BY date_column ROWS BETWEEN 6 PRECEDING AND CURRENT ROW). This smooths daily fluctuations and highlights longer trends. If you're dealing with dates, make sure the ORDER BY uses a real date or datetime, not just a textual label.

Step 4: Add a centered moving average for smoothing. A centered 3-day average uses ROWS BETWEEN 1 PRECEDING AND 1 FOLLOWING. It looks at the day before and after the current day, which can produce a gentler line in charts. Think of this as looking around the current point to sense the local trend.

Step 5: Combine moving averages with other metrics. You can layer a moving average on top of a running total or a cumulative metric to reveal both scale and slope. For example, you might calculate a

7-day moving average of daily revenue and also track the cumulative revenue up to each day with a separate window frame.

Step 6: Test with real data and watch for edge cases. On the first days of a dataset, a moving average will have fewer preceding points, so some SQL engines return NULLs for the first few days. You can handle this by starting the window a day later or by using COALESCE to substitute a fallback value. This keeps your charts clean and your reports consistent.

Two practical micro-cases for frame clauses. Micro-case A: You have daily temperatures and want a 7-day moving average to spot gradual shifts without daily noise. Micro-case B: You're tracing daily sales and also want a centered 3-day average to smooth the line around holidays when data may drop.

Event sequencing, gaps-and-islands and sessionization techniques

Step 1: Define what counts as sequencing. Event sequencing focuses on the order of events, such as user actions or sensor readings. The goal is to understand how actions unfold over time, not just what happened.

Step 2: Detect gaps between events. Use LAG to bring in the previous timestamp for each user or item, and compute the difference to see how long the gap was. A large gap often signals a new phase, a break, or a separate session.

Step 3: Identify gaps and islands. Islands are continuous runs of events with small gaps; gaps are the breaks that separate those runs. A common trick uses a difference between a date (or timestamp) and a row number to group consecutive events into islands. When the difference stays the same, you're in the same island; when it changes, a new island starts.

Step 4: Assign session identifiers. After identifying gaps, you can assign a session_id by counting how many gaps have occurred within a user's event stream up to each row. A running total that increments when the gap threshold is exceeded creates a handy session label you can use for analysis.

Step 5: Sessionize with thresholds. Decide what counts as a session break. A typical threshold is 30 minutes of inactivity, but you can tailor it to your data and goals. The exact value isn't magic; it's a policy that makes your analytics meaningful for your scenario.

Step 6: Apply the ideas to real logs. For a web site, you might sessionize by user_id and time between clicks. For a sensor network, you might identify sessions when readings arrive within a short, regular cadence and separate them when the cadence pauses.

Two concrete micro-cases you can explore. Micro-case A: A user's activity log shows multiple actions; you define sessions where a 20-minute gap ends a session and a new one begins, then tally the number of sessions per user. Micro-case B: A device sends readings every minute, but bursts occur; you identify bursts as islands of activity separated by more than 5 minutes and count how many bursts each device produces in a day.

Key Takeaway: Window functions let you describe how data behaves over time within defined groups, not just how many rows you have. They can rank, smooth, and organize events in ways that ordinary aggregates can't.

Coming up next Subtittle: Subqueries, CTEs and Derived Tables

1) Correlated versus uncorrelated subqueries and their performance trade-offs

2) Common Table Expressions (CTEs) and recursive queries for hierarchical data

3) Refactoring subqueries into joins and materialized intermediates

Chapter 4

Subqueries, CTEs and Derived Tables

You will be able to use correlated and uncorrelated subqueries effectively, write recursive CTEs for hierarchical data, and refactor subqueries into joins or materialized intermediates to simplify and speed up your SQL.

Correlated versus uncorrelated subqueries: what they are and why they matter

Think of a subquery as a little question inside a bigger question. An uncorrelated subquery asks a question that doesn't depend on the outer row being examined. It can often be answered once and reused, which makes it a good candidate for optimization and caching. A correlated subquery, by contrast, asks a question that depends on data from the row you're currently looking at. The inner question changes as you move from row to row. This can be powerful, but it also tends to be more demanding on your database, because the inner query might run many times.

Step 1. Identify which subqueries you're using. Look for inner queries that reference columns from the outer query. If you see that linkage, you're likely dealing with a correlated subquery. If the inner query stands alone, not using any column from the outer query, it's likely uncorrelated.

Step 2. Gauge the performance signal. Correlated subqueries often run for every row, which can lead to slow queries on large tables. Uncorrelated subqueries can often be optimized by the database engine, especially if the inner query is small or can be computed as a hash join, a compute, or a pre-aggregated result.

Step 3. Try a rewrite when you can. If you have a correlated subquery that essentially filters by a computed value from the inner table, see if a join or an exists check can achieve the same result with less repetition. The goal is to reduce the number of times the inner logic runs.

Step 4. Be mindful of the data distribution. If the inner query uses a field that's highly selective and indexed, a correlated form may still be fine. If not, a rewrite often wins. Always test with realistic data sizes and measure execution time and plan shapes.

Two concrete examples illustrate the idea

Example A: An uncorrelated subquery

Suppose you want to find customers who have made any purchase above a certain threshold. The inner question can stand alone: what is the threshold, and which purchases exceed it? You can write a query that checks each customer against the precomputed set of large purchases. For instance, select customers where the customer_id appears in a subquery that selects customer_ids from orders where amount exceeds a fixed threshold. This subquery doesn’t refer to the outer customers table and can be evaluated once, or even optimized away, depending on the optimizer.

Example B: A correlated subquery

Now imagine you want customers who have at least one order above a threshold. The inner query must see the current outer customer_id to decide if there's a qualifying order. A typical pattern uses EXISTS or IN with a correlated subquery. EXISTS tests existentials efficiently, often allowing the engine to stop early once it finds a match. The trade-off is clear: you gain precise, row-by-row filtering, but you pay for repeated inner evaluations if there are many customers and many orders.

Where to apply the rewrite

- When a subquery is repeatedly evaluated across many outer rows, check if a join can express the same logic more directly.

- If the inner query is independent of the outer row, favor uncorrelated forms and flattening into a single plan with a join or a set operation.

- If you rely on scalar values from the inner query for each outer row, test a correlated EXISTS pattern or a join-based approach that returns the same boolean result more efficiently.

Common table expressions and recursive queries: turning complexity into clarity

CTEs are named temporary result sets that you define once and can reuse within the same query. They can dramatically improve readability and maintainability, especially for long queries that mix filters, calculations, and subqueries. Recursive CTEs take that idea further, letting you walk through hierarchical data such as organization charts, product categories, or threaded discussions.

Step 1. Start with a simple, readable CTE. Name the CTE and define it with a clear purpose, such as filtering a base dataset, computing an aggregate, or isolating a tricky join. The outer query then reads like a story: “From this clean, named set, perform the next step.” This makes complex logic much easier to follow.

Step 2. Move to recursion only when there’s a real hierarchy to traverse. A recursive CTE has two parts: an anchor member (the starting rows) and a recursive member (how you step from one level to the next). The recursion ends when no new rows are produced. Use termination conditions carefully to avoid infinite loops.

Step 3. Keep the recursion bounded and safe. Include a maximum depth guard if you expect deep trees, or rely on the database's built-in safeguards. Always test with the deepest expected level to ensure the query finishes in a reasonable time.

Step 4. Weigh readability against performance. Simple, well-structured CTEs often perform as well as or better than long nested subqueries. But recursive queries can be heavier. In some cases, materializing part of the result with a non-recursive CTE or a temporary table helps.

Two practical micro-cases

Micro-case 1: Simple non-recursive CTE for clarity

Suppose you need to select orders in a date range and compute a running total for each day. A CTE can first isolate the relevant orders, then a second step computes daily totals. The final query reads like a sequence of logical steps, not a wall of nested logic. This clarity often helps you spot mistakes, or opportunities to optimize with indexes or partitioning.

Micro-case 2: Recursive CTE for hierarchical data

Imagine you have a table of employees with manager_id linking to the same table. A recursive CTE can build a full reporting line for a given manager. The anchor picks the direct reports, the recursive step adds the next level up, and the recursion stops when no new people appear. The resulting set gives you the complete tree path for each employee, making questions like "who reports to whom" straightforward to answer.

Refactoring subqueries into joins and materialized intermediates

Sometimes the cleanest, fastest path is to stop asking a subquery every time and instead materialize its results, then join to that intermediate result. This can reduce repeated work and give the optimizer a clearer plan.

Step 1. Identify opportunities to replace subqueries with joins. If a subquery returns a small, fixed set that can be joined on a common key, a join often performs better because the database engine can use indexes and optimized join strategies.

Step 2. Convert IN or EXISTS subqueries to joins where possible. For example, turning a subquery that filters with IN (SELECT id FROM table) into a join on the table's id can improve readability and speed, especially when the subquery is uncorrelated or semi-structured. The same logic applies to EXISTS, which can sometimes be rewritten as a semi-join.

Step 3. Use derived tables or materialized intermediates for heavy computations. If you have a costly subquery that you must reuse across multiple parts of a larger query, pull it out into a derived table or a CTE and reference that intermediate. This makes the plan easier to optimize and can help with caching and reusing results.

Step 4. Be mindful of the trade-offs. Materializing intermediates can reduce repeated work but adds a named step in the plan. It can also require more memory or I/O. Test with real data sizes to see where the sweet spot lies.

Two practical refactor examples

Example C: Refactoring a WHERE x IN (SELECT y FROM z) into a join

Original: select a.* from a where a.x in (select y from z where condition);

Refactored: select a.* from a join z on a.x = z.y where z.condition;

The join version often allows the optimizer to apply better access methods and push predicates into the right places, improving performance and making the intent clearer.

Example D: Using a derived table to reuse a heavy calculation

Original: select t1.*, (select sum(v) from t2 where t2.k = t1.k) as total from t1;

If you compute that sum once and reuse it, you can write: with calc as (select k, sum(v) as total from t2 group by k) select t1.*, calc.total from t1 join calc on t1.k = calc.k;

This pattern avoids repeating the sum calculation for each row and helps the planner optimize the rest of the query.

Common pitfalls and quick fixes

- Pitfall: leaning too heavily on correlated subqueries because they feel precise. Fix: test a join-based alternative; you may gain speed without losing correctness.

- Pitfall: recursive CTEs that never terminate. Fix: always include a termination condition and test with the maximum expected depth.

- Pitfall: over-materializing. Fix: measure impact; sometimes small intermediates are enough, and minimal materialization keeps memory usage reasonable.

- Pitfall: poor indexing on join keys. Fix: ensure relevant keys in both sides of the join are indexed or partitioned for better plan choices.

Key Takeaway: When you see a subquery, ask three questions: Is it correlated? Can I rewrite it with a join? Do I gain clarity or speed by extracting an intermediate? Answering these helps you write queries that are easier to read and faster to run.

Coming up next Subtittle: Advanced Aggregation and Grouping Techniques

1) ROLLUP, CUBE and GROUPING SETS for multi-dimensional summaries

2) Filtered aggregates, conditional aggregation and pivoting strategies

3) Designing aggregation pipelines for reporting and analytics

Coming up next

You'll build on what you learned here by exploring shapes of data beyond single-row results and into multi-dimensional summaries. You'll see how to summarize data across many angles, refine results with filters, and design pipelines that feed dashboards and reports with powerful, scalable queries. As you move into the next chapter, keep an eye on how your new understanding of subqueries and CTEs can simplify the aggregation patterns you'll encounter, and how recursion and intermediate results can simplify complex reporting tasks.

Chapter 5

Advanced Aggregation and Grouping Techniques

By the end of this chapter, you will be able to create multi-dimensional totals with rollups, cubes, and grouping sets, turn rows into pivots with conditional aggregation, and design clear aggregation pipelines that support real-world reporting and analytics.

Rollup, Cube and Grouping Sets

You already know how to group data by a single set of columns. Now you'll learn to add layers of totals without writing a dozen separate queries. Rollup, cube, and grouping sets are tools that let you ask for several related groupings in one statement. Rollup creates a hierarchical path of totals—think totals by product, then by category, then a grand total. Cube goes wider: it produces all possible combinations of the listed groupings, so you can see every intersection of those categories and their totals. Grouping sets are the most precise of the three: you pick the exact combinations you want, from simple to complex, and you get only those totals. None of these are mysterious tricks.

They're just different ways to slice the data so you can see patterns at multiple levels at once.

Two quick micro-cases help make this concrete. Micro-case one: you have a sales table with region, product, and amount. You want totals by region and product, totals by region alone, totals by product alone, and a grand total. A single grouping sets clause can produce all of these: group by grouping sets ((region, product), (region), (product), ()). When you run it, you'll see some rows with region and product filled in and others with NULLs in the places where that level of detail isn't being reported. The NULLs aren't errors; they mark the levels that don't apply to that row.

Micro-case two expands the view: you want every combination of region, product, and year, plus the overall totals. A cube lets you do that automatically, giving you the full grid of all region/product/year intersections, plus the corners where some values are missing in the grid and flagged as NULL. If your data uses more dimensions, grouping sets give you similar control but with exact precision over which totals you want.

A practical example helps seal the idea. Imagine a table named sales with columns region, product, year, and amount. A simple query using grouping sets could look like this: select region, product, year, sum(amount) as total_sales from sales group by grouping sets ((region, product, year), (region, product), (region, year), (product, year), (region), (product), (year), ()) . The result is a matrix of rows: every combination you asked for, plus the grand total. You'll see how totals stack up at different levels of detail, and you'll be able to spot which parts of your data drive the totals and where gaps appear.

Rollup and cube are especially handy when you're building reports for monitors, dashboards, or executive summaries. They let you avoid writing a dozen separate queries to get the same information at varying levels. Grouping sets gives you the exact tailor-made set of totals you need, without extra clutter or repeated logic. The core idea to keep in mind: these tools are about multi-level totals and combinational summaries, not about making data harder to read. They make patterns clearer, and that clarity pays off in faster decisions.

Pivoting and conditionality naturally fit with these techniques. You may want to see totals by region and by product, with a grand total at the end. You can combine grouping sets with conditional aggregation to show exactly what you need in each line of the report, nudging NULLs into place where a level doesn't apply. The key is to plan the levels you want before you write the query, then let the grouping mechanism assemble the right rows for you.

Transitioning to the next idea, you'll see how to sharpen results with filtered aggregates and pivoting. This helps you extract the precise signals you care about from a large dataset, even before you apply any broader company-wide reporting techniques.

Filtered Aggregates, Conditional Aggregation and Pivoting Strategies

Filtered aggregates are a clean way to compute several views of the same data without running multiple queries. Instead of pulling a separate subset into a subquery, you attach the filter directly to the aggregate. You can use a FILTER clause in some systems, or you can run a single aggregate with a CASE expression. The principle is simple: pick the rows you want for each calculation, then sum, count, or average them.

Two practical micro-cases illustrate the idea. Micro-case one: you want total sales and total discounted sales by region. You have a column discount_flag that marks discounted transactions. Using a CASE expression, you can do a single grouping by region, with two sums inside: SUM(amount) for all sales, and SUM(CASE WHEN discount_flag = true THEN amount ELSE 0 END) for discounted sales. The result shows both totals side by side for every region, without needing two separate queries.

Micro-case two demonstrates pivoting with conditional aggregation. Suppose you want to see, for each product, the sales totals in three regions: North, South, and West. You can create a single row per product with three columns: total for North, total for South, and total for West. The query uses conditional sums like SUM(CASE WHEN region = 'North' THEN amount ELSE 0 END) AS North, and similarly for the other regions. If you add more regions, you simply add more columns in the same pattern. This is a practical pivoting approach that works in many databases without special pivot syntax.

A more elegant version uses the FILTER clause available in some systems: SUM(amount) FILTER (WHERE discount_flag = true) AS discounted_total. This keeps the logic compact and expressive. If your database supports FILTER, you get clean syntax; if not, the CASE version is a reliable, portable alternative. Either way, the goal is the same: produce multiple views from a single pass through the data, which reduces work, speeds up iteration, and minimizes the chance of mismatched results across reports.

Pivoting strategies aren't limited to tiny tables. If you're reporting on yearly performance across many regions and products, conditional aggregation scales well. You can combine it with a rollup to create a multi-level matrix: you could compute region totals across all products, then drill down into product-level totals within each region, culminating in an overall grand total. The trick is to keep your expressions readable and to document the reasoning behind each column. That way, someone reviewing the report later can understand what each number represents without rereading the entire query.

As you practice, remember a few common patterns. Use CASE or FILTER to separate data by category, time period, or dimension, then apply the aggregate you need—SUM, AVG, COUNT, or others. When you combine several of these, you get a compact, readable, and fast way to produce dashboards and reports. If a particular pivot feels brittle, double-check that you're grouping on the right columns and that your conditional expressions cover all possible values (including the edge cases where a region or category might be missing in some rows).

Transitioning now to how to assemble these ideas into a practical workflow, you'll learn how to design aggregation pipelines that prepare data for analytics and reporting without getting lost in a tangle of subqueries.

Designing Aggregation Pipelines for Reporting and Analytics

An aggregation pipeline is a sequence of steps that progressively refines data into a final, readable result set. Think of it as a production line: each stage takes the output of the previous stage and adds a new layer of meaning or a new level of summarization. You typically implement pipelines with a series of subqueries or with common table expressions (CTEs). The result is clearer logic, easier maintenance, and better performance if you structure it well.

In practice, you start with Stage 1: a straightforward grouping on the most granular level you care about. For example, you might aggregate by date, region, and product, producing daily totals per region and product. Stage 1 establishes the baseline numbers you'll build on.

Stage 2 adds a layer of summarization. Here you group Stage 1 results into larger baskets—perhaps weekly totals by region, or monthly totals by product. This stage turns many small pieces into bigger stories, and you can push the grouping down to the level that your reporting needs require. It's common to keep the first-stage details available as a reference in case someone needs to drill back into the original data.

Stage 3 ties things together for final reports. You can apply a final grouping to produce high-level dashboards, such as regional totals by month, or product totals by quarter, with a grand total at the end. This stage often uses one of the multi-level grouping techniques discussed earlier (ROLLUP, CUBE, or GROUPING SETS) to deliver a table that reads like a matrix of useful summaries.

A short, concrete example helps. Suppose you have a sales table with date, region, product, and amount. Stage 1 could compute daily totals by region and product. Stage 2 could roll those up to weekly totals by region, preserving the region and product dimensions. Stage 3 could then summarize by region across all products for each week, and finally produce an overall weekly total. You'd store the results of each stage in a CTE or a subquery so each step is explicit and auditable. This approach also makes it easy to re-run the pipeline with different dates or regions, which is handy for month-to-date or quarter-to-date reporting.

An important practical tip: keep the pipeline modular. If you later need a slightly different final view—say, a pivot that shows regions as columns and weeks as rows—you should be able to adjust only the final stage or add another stage, without rewriting the entire chain. That modularity makes debugging much easier and reduces the risk of introducing inconsistency across reports.

Another helpful pattern is to document each stage with a brief comment in your SQL or a separate design note. Note what the stage does, what inputs it expects, and what the output looks like. Clear documentation helps teammates, managers, and future you understand why a certain aggregation was built a particular way and how to reuse it for new questions.

As you practice, you'll balance two things: precision and performance. More stages and more grouping can give you richer reports, but they can also slow down the query. Start with the simplest pipeline that satisfies the reporting need, then profile and optimize. If you see bottlenecks, consider materializing intermediate results or narrowing data with early filters before you aggregate. These choices depend on your data size, how your database optimizer behaves, and what you need to deliver in a given timeframe.

Key Takeaway: Multi-dimensional totals, conditional aggregations, and well-constructed pipelines let you turn large datasets into clear, actionable insights without drowning in complexity.

Coming up next

Subtittle: Query Optimization and Indexing

1) Designing effective indexes: composite, covering and expression-based keys,

2) Understanding statistics, cardinality estimation and optimizer choices,

3) Query rewrite, plan stabilization and judicious use of optimizer hints

Chapter 6

Query Optimization and Indexing

You will learn how to design effective indexes, understand statistics that guide your plans, and rewrite queries for stability.

Designing effective indexes: composite, covering and expression-based keys

Indexes are road signs for your database. They tell the engine where to find data quickly. When you design an index, you're choosing which columns the database should sort and locate first. Three kinds of indexes you'll rely on are composite indexes, covering indexes, and expression-based indexes. Each type helps in different situations, so you'll often combine them to match the exact shape of your queries.

Step 1. Map your hot queries. Start by listing the queries you run most often, especially those that fetch large tables or return small results after filtering. Look for patterns: do you filter by several columns at once? Do you sort by a column or a combination of columns? Do you only need a few columns from a wide table? The more you understand the filters, the better you can align an index with how you actually search the data. The goal is to put the most selective filters first in the index key, so the database can quickly narrow down to a small subset.

Rationale: The order of columns in a composite index matters. A query that filters on column A and then B will be fastest if the index starts with A and then B. If your query also sorts on B, having B in the index helps avoid extra lookups. This is the core idea behind composite indexes: they combine multiple search paths into one, so the engine can use a single structure to locate rows.

Step 2. Build a composite index that matches filters and sorting. Create a single index that mirrors the common filter sequence and, if possible, the sort order your query uses. If you regularly filter by region and date, consider an index on (region, date). If you frequently filter by region and status and return a handful of columns, you might make an index on (region, status) and ensure the needed columns are covered by including them in the index.

Rationale: The design should minimize the number of data fetches. A well-ordered composite index can make the search faster and reduce the need to read actual table rows. If your queries often read only a few columns, you can extend the index to include those columns as covered columns. A covering index is like a cheat sheet: it has all the data a query reads, so the engine can answer from the index alone without touching the table.

Step 3. Use expression-based and included columns when needed. If you frequently search with a transformed value, like a case-insensitive email lookup, an index on the expression (for example, lower(email)) can save work. If your database supports including non-key columns in the index, add the SELECTed columns there so the engine can return data directly from the index.

Rationale: Expression-based indexes let you turn common but awkward filters into fast lookups.

Including columns in an index can turn an index lookup into a complete answer without extra lookups, which can dramatically reduce I/O and latency.

Two micro-cases to illustrate

Micro-case 1: A sales table with frequent regional filtering and date-range queries. You often run:

```
SELECT sale_id, amount

FROM sales

WHERE region = 'West'
```

```
AND sale_date >= '2024-01-01'
ORDER BY sale_date DESC
LIMIT 100;
```

A strong choice would be a composite index on (region, sale_date) with sale_id and amount included (or as covered columns). This alignment means the database can quickly locate rows in the West region, then narrow by date, and finally return the required columns without additional lookups. The result is a visibly faster, more predictable response as the data grows.

Micro-case 2: A user table with a common case-insensitive search on email. You run:

```
SELECT user_id, name
FROM users
WHERE LOWER(email) =
'student@example.org';
```

Here an index on the expression LOWER(email) supports the query directly. If your system supports it, you can also create a small covering index that includes user_id and name to avoid reading the main table after locating the matching rows.

What to watch for

- Don't over-index. Each index adds maintenance cost on writes. If a query doesn't need a fast read path, adding an index may slow down inserts, updates, and deletes.

- Align index order with how you filter, group, or sort. If a query filters on A and B but sorts on B, the index order that starts with A and then B is usually better.

- Test with real workloads. Use explain plans or query plans to verify that the engine uses the index you expect. If it doesn't, reexamine the filter order, index coverage, or included columns.

Understanding statistics, cardinality estimation and optimizer choices

Statistics describe your data in broad terms. They tell the database how many rows match a filter, how data is distributed, and how costly different access paths might be. The optimizer uses these statistics to choose an execution plan—whether to use index scans, table scans, joins, or different join orders. When statistics are out of date, the optimizer can pick slower plans even for queries that previously ran fast.

Step 4. Know the role statistics play in plan choices. Statistics include row counts and distributions. If most of your data has a certain value, the optimizer may expect a high selectivity for that value and choose one plan, while if data is evenly distributed, it may choose another. The key idea is that the optimizer makes educated guesses based on what it knows about the data.

Rationale: Plans are chosen to minimize estimated cost. If the estimates are close to reality, you'll see efficient execution. When estimates are off, you can see surprises like a slow full scan where an index was expected to be used.

Step 5. Keep statistics fresh. Data changes over time. New rows, deleted rows, or updated distributions can shift the best plan. Maintaining statistics regularly helps the optimizer stay aligned with reality. In many systems, you can trigger statistics updates automatically or on a schedule.

After updating, re-check the plan to confirm the change in behavior.

Rationale: Fresh statistics reduce the chance of a poor plan caused by stale data. In dynamic datasets, keeping stats current is one of the easiest wins for performance reliability.

Step 6. Watch cardinality and learn how it guides plans. Cardinality is the term for how many rows a condition will return. High-cardinality columns (many unique values) can often be referenced efficiently with indexes. Low-cardinality columns (few unique values) sometimes benefit from different strategies, such as rewriting queries or using different indexes. If your query's predicates target a column with low cardinality, the optimizer might lean toward a different access method than you expect.

Rationale: Understanding whether your filters are high- or low-cardinality helps you design better indexes and set expectations for query speed. When your guess about cardinality is off, even a good index may not perform as well as you hoped.

Two micro-cases to illustrate

Micro-case A: A product catalog where a filter on category_id returns many rows. If the filter is not very selective, a simple index on category_id may not help much by itself. But pairing category_id with another selective column (like price_range or availability) in a composite index can improve selectivity and speed.

Micro-case B: A user table that has rapidly changing data such as last_login_date. Statistics show many users share the same last_login_date when you look at small time windows, so an index on last_login_date might not always be helpful. Here, you may rely more on query rewriting and selective filters on higher-cardinality columns to speed up common lookups.

Query rewrite, plan stabilization and judicious use of optimizer hints

Sometimes the fastest path is not the obvious one. You can rewrite queries to encourage the optimizer to choose better plans, stabilize plans to avoid unwanted changes between runs, and use hints to nudge the engine when you are confident about the best approach.

Step 7. Rewrite subqueries into joins when it helps. If a query uses a subquery to filter results, consider whether a join could express the same logic more efficiently. Joins often enable the optimizer to use indexes more effectively and avoid materializing subquery results. In practice, a well-chosen join order can transform a slow query into a fast, streaming one.

Rationale: Joins give the optimizer more flexibility in planning access paths. A subtler benefit is that joins often map nicely to how data is stored and indexed, reducing the need for repeated lookups.

Step 8. Stabilize plans with consistent patterns and prepared statements. If your workload shows plan volatility—where the same query slowly performs differently across runs—try to use parameterized queries or prepared statements.

When the engine sees the same shape of query with different literal values, it can choose a consistent plan instead of recomputing one each time.

Rationale: Plan stability reduces unpredictable performance swings. It's especially helpful for reporting dashboards or scheduled jobs that run often with different values but the same structure.

Step 9. Use optimizer hints cautiously and as a last resort. Hints can tell the optimizer to prefer a certain index, join method, or join order. They can rescue a stubborn query, but they can also mislead the optimizer as data grows or changes. When you use hints, monitor performance and be ready to remove them if they start to cause regressions.

Rationale: Hints bypass normal optimization rules. They are powerful but can lock you into a suboptimal path as data evolves. Use them only after you've verified that the default plan is consistently worse, and you've tested under representative workloads.

Two micro-cases to illustrate

Micro-case C: A critical report that always runs on a large table. The query plan initially uses a full table scan. After rewriting the query to use a targeted index path and, if supported by your system, applying a mild hint to prefer an index path, the report runs in a fraction of the time.

Micro-case D: A complex analytic query that joins several large tables. The optimizer chooses a reasonable plan most of the time, but on particular data shapes it errodes. You can rewrite one subquery into a join and rely on a stable, well-indexed path, then validate results with a simple test set and compare runtimes.

Key Takeaway: Align your indexes with how you search, keep statistics fresh so plans stay accurate, and use careful rewrites and hints to keep critical queries fast without sacrificing reliability.

Coming up next: Subtittle: Transactions, Concurrency and Reliability

You'll explore ACID principles and how to pick isolation levels, learn how locking works and how to detect and resolve contention, and discover safe patterns for savepoints and retries in long-running transactions. This will help you keep data safe while you push performance higher, so you can design systems that are both fast and dependable.

Chapter 7

Transactions, Concurrency and Reliability

By the end of this chapter you will be able to design transaction flows that keep data safe, handle locking and contention, and use savepoints and retry logic to finish long-running work without breaking rules of data integrity.

ACID principles and selecting appropriate isolation levels

ACID is a short way to remember four promises your database makes every time you run a transaction. Atomicity means “all or nothing.” If a bank transfer happens, both sides must update or neither should. Consistency means the data stays valid according to the rules you’ve set. If you have a rule that prevents negative balances, that rule must still hold after the transaction finishes. Isolation means transactions don’t smear into each other. What you read during a transaction should reflect a consistent snapshot unless you’re willing to accept some changes as the transaction progresses. Durability means once a transaction is committed, it stays there, even if something bad happens right after.

In the real world, you choose how strictly to enforce those promises by picking an isolation level. Think of isolation levels as different ways to guard the data while many things change around it. The simplest level, often called “low isolation,” may let you see uncommitted changes from others (a dirty read) and can lead to confusing results. A mid-level level prevents you from seeing uncommitted changes, which helps most apps, but you can still encounter changes when you read the same data twice in one transaction (non-repeatable reads). A higher level protects you from those surprises, but it can slow things down because the system blocks more aggressively to keep data pristine. The highest level aims for a perfectly predictable view of data, but it usually means more waiting for locks to clear and more time for each transaction to finish.

When should you pick each level? If you're building something where mistakes are costly and you need every read to be stable, you'll lean toward higher isolation. If you're building a fast, heavy-traffic system where some minor inconsistencies are tolerable during processing, a lower isolation level can help you scale. The right choice often comes down to your data's criticality and how long you're willing to wait for locks.

Two short micro-cases help make this concrete. First, imagine you're implementing a simple wallet transfer between two users. You need both the debit and the credit to happen together. If you read the balances, then decide what to debit, and someone else updates a balance in the middle, you could end up with a tiny mismatch. A higher isolation level helps prevent that, because the system makes sure the balances you see don't change mid-transaction. Second, consider a shopping cart that reads stock levels and then places an order. If another user buys the last item while you're still reading, you could either overcommit or show an item as available when it's not. A careful isolation choice or a way to lock the stock record until the order completes can prevent that kind of conflict.

Practical patterns to keep in mind: define a clear boundary for what a transaction is allowed to do; treat multiple, related reads and writes as a single unit; test under scenarios that mimic real user loads to see how your chosen isolation level behaves. I've seen teams save themselves a lot of trouble by starting with a sensible default (like Read Committed in many systems) and then tightening only where tests reveal a real risk of anomalies. Remember, you can often improve performance without sacrificing safety by restructuring the transaction so it holds locks for less time.

Two tiny examples show the idea in action. In the first, a transfer between two accounts reads both balances, then updates them. If the system pauses halfway and another transfer begins, you could end up with inconsistent totals unless the isolation level protects reads and the write path is atomic. In the second example, an inventory check followed by a purchase could misreport stock if another purchase happens at the exact same moment. Using a higher isolation level or locking the stock row for the duration of the check-and-update can prevent that misstep. The key is to decide what level of wobble you'll tolerate and then design the code paths to stay within that boundary.

Locking behavior, detecting contention and resolving deadlocks

To keep data safe, the database uses locks. Locks are signals that say, “Only this transaction may change this piece of data right now.” They can happen at different levels: a single row, a set of rows, or an entire page or table. Locks prevent two transactions from stomping on each other’s changes at the same moment. That protection is essential, but it can become a headache if two transactions lock things in different orders and end up waiting forever for each other. That situation is a deadlock.

Most modern databases handle locking automatically and detect deadlocks. When a deadlock is detected, the database will choose one of the transactions to abort and roll back, then the other one can proceed. As a developer, you don't get to control which side wins; you prepare for the possibility and make your code resilient.

A few practical patterns help you avoid lock fights and deadlocks. First, keep transactions short. The less time you hold locks, the less likely you are to collide with others. Second, access resources in a consistent order. If every operation always touches, say, user rows before order rows, two concurrent processes won't get stuck in opposite orders. Third, minimize the data touched in a transaction. If you can narrow the scope to just the necessary rows, you reduce the chance of locking conflicts. Fourth, consider using a lower isolation level when safe, or rely on optimistic approaches where you detect conflicts after you've tried updates and retry if a conflict is found. Fifth, catch and handle deadlock errors gracefully, often by retrying the transaction after a short pause.

Two short scenarios illustrate the point. Scenario A shows two processes trying to update two rows: A updates a balance, then B updates a stock item. If A locks the balance row first and B locks the stock row first, and both need the other's lock to complete, a deadlock can occur. If you design the code so both processes always access balance first and then stock, the deadlock risk drops dramatically. Scenario B involves a batch job that updates many rows in a table. If multiple workers attempt the same rows in parallel, you can create contention that slows everything down. The remedy is often to distribute workload more evenly, lock fewer rows per operation, or queue work so only one worker handles a given slice at a time.

When contention does happen, retries become your friend. The trick is to make retries predictable and safe. Use short delays between attempts, and consider a small backoff strategy so you don't hammer the system. Make sure your retry logic is idempotent—doing the same operation twice should not cause a different result than doing it once. That often means treating the operation as a sequence of steps that can be safely repeated from a known point.

Two micro-cases bring this to life. In the first, two users attempt to place a bid on the same item at almost the same time. A lock collision might force one bid to wait, then retry. If the system is designed to retry quickly but intelligently, the second attempt will succeed without creating inconsistent state. In the second case, a financial reconciliation process locks a summary row, reads several detailed lines, and updates totals. If another process holds the same summary row, the second process should back off and retry, rather than forcing the first to release its lock in an awkward moment.

Savepoints, retry logic and strategies for long-running transactional work

Savepoints are like bookmarks inside a long transaction. They let you roll back just part of a transaction if something goes wrong, while still keeping the rest of the work intact. This is especially useful when a transaction has multiple steps that could fail independently, such as creating an order, charging a payment, and updating inventory. Instead of rolling back the entire transaction when one step fails, you can roll back to a safe savepoint and retry only the failing part. This often saves time and keeps data consistent without starting over.

Retry logic is your safety net for long-running work. When a transaction might take a long time or encounter temporary contention, retrying ensures you don't lose progress due to a momentary hiccup. The best retry strategies use short delays between attempts and an upper limit on retries. You want to avoid a loop that never ends or that floods the system with repeated attempts. A practical approach is to cap how many times you retry, and after that, surface a clear error for human review or automated escalation.

A concrete workflow helps students grasp the idea. Suppose you're processing a large order with three steps: reserve inventory, charge payment, and confirm the order. You can place a savepoint after reserving inventory. If charging the payment fails due to a temporary issue, you roll back to the savepoint rather than undoing the inventory reservation. Then you retry charging the payment a few times with short delays. If it finally succeeds, you complete the rest of the steps. If it never succeeds after the retries, you roll back to the very beginning of the transaction, but you've preserved the ability to skip unnecessary rework and re-run from a clearer point.

Two short examples make this vivid. Example one shows a long-running batch that processes many accounts. It uses a savepoint after every hundred accounts so that if a problem crops up mid-batch, you don't have to restart the entire batch—just the current chunk. Example two shows a payment gateway that occasionally hiccups. The process saves a point before charging, retries a few times with backoff, and only if all retries fail does it escalate, leaving the rest of the transaction untouched and recoverable.

Key Takeaway: Use ACID thinking to frame each transaction, pick an isolation level that balances safety with performance, keep locks short, and design with savepoints and measured retries so long tasks don't derail data integrity.

Coming up next Subtittle: Stored Procedures, Functions and Triggers

1) Designing modular stored procedures with clear parameter and error conventions,

2) Scalar, inline and table-valued functions: behavior and performance implications,

3) Trigger types, safe usage patterns and avoiding unintended side effects

Chapter 8

Stored Procedures, Functions and Triggers

You will design modular stored procedures, understand the three main kinds of user-defined functions, and use triggers safely to keep your database reliable and easy to maintain.

1) Designing modular stored procedures with clear parameter and error conventions

Start with a strong contract. A stored procedure should have a focused job, a clear list of inputs, and a simple way to return results or status. Name parameters in a way that describes what they are for, not how you plan to use them inside. Decide which data must arrive (inputs) and which results you should hand back (outputs or a status code). Treat inputs as commitments: validate them early, reject bad data, and fail gracefully instead of letting errors cascade.

Keep the core logic clean and small. A good rule is: one procedure should do one thing well, and it should call other helpers only when that makes the job easier to test and reuse. Avoid embedding long, complicated routines inside a single procedure. If you can, split heavy computations or data checks into separate, testable units and call them from the main procedure. This separation makes debugging faster and keeps future changes from breaking other parts of your system.

Handle errors in a predictable way. Use a consistent method for signaling success or failure. This could mean returning a status code, or using an OUTPUT parameter to convey a new ID or a descriptive message. When something goes wrong, capture the problem with a descriptive message and avoid swallowing the error. If your environment supports it, a TRY...CATCH block is a reliable way to catch exceptions and surface a clean error to the caller.

Document the contract and changes. Leave a short description at the top of the procedure, list each parameter with its purpose, data type, and any constraints. When you update the procedure, add a CHANGE LOG note so future readers know what changed and why. This practice saves time and reduces mistakes for you and anyone else who uses your code later.

Two practical micro-cases illuminate the ideas.

Micro-case A: RegisterNewUser

Goal: add a new user to the system, returning the new user ID and a status.

What you do: define inputs like @Username, @Email, @RoleId, and an OUTPUT parameter @NewUserId; optionally return a status message. Validate inputs (e.g., ensure username isn't already taken, email looks plausible). In the core logic, perform the insert and capture the new ID, then return it through the OUTPUT parameter and a success status.

Rationale: this demonstrates a clean contract, input validation, and a deterministic result that callers can rely on. It also shows how to expose useful results without leaking internal details or side effects into other parts of the application.

Micro-case B: GetUserCountByRole

Goal: return the count of users in each role without exposing full user data.

What you do: create a small procedure that accepts a role filter (optional) and returns a compact result set or a single count value. Keep the logic simple and readable. Avoid mixing heavy data-fetching code with business rules in the same place.

Rationale: this shows how modular procedures can provide focused capabilities and be combined with other procedures to build bigger workflows without duplicating logic.

A compact template you can adapt

Procedure contract template (conceptual, not literal code):

- Purpose: describe what the procedure does in one line.

- Parameters: list @Name (type, direction IN/OUT, constraints), with clear validation rules.

- Returns: specify either an OUTPUT value or a result set and a status.

- Error handling: outline how errors are surfaced (e.g., error codes and messages).

- Side effects: note any data changes or external actions.

- Testing notes: quick checks to verify the contract.

Checklist for design

- Is the procedure focused on a single task?

- Are inputs clearly named and validated early?

- Is output signaling consistent across procedures?

- Can the logic be tested in isolation?

- Is there a concise change log or comments describing updates?

2) Scalar, inline and table-valued functions: behavior and performance implications

Understand the three main kinds of functions and why their behavior matters in real systems.

Scalar functions: these return a single value. They are easy to use in SELECT lists or predicates, but they can incur performance costs if run for many rows. In many databases, scalar functions execute row by row, which can slow queries that touch large datasets. Use scalar functions for straightforward, well-optimized calculations or lookups that don't require heavy data access. If you can, push logic into the main query (as joins or inline expressions) or replace scalar functions with inline table-valued functions when performance matters.

Inline table-valued functions (ITVF): these return a table based on a single SELECT statement. They combine the readability of a function with the set-based power of a query, and they usually perform better than scalar functions because they're optimized like a regular query plan. Use ITVF when you need to expose a reusable, parameterized view of data without returning a scalar value.

Table-valued functions (TVF) in general: there are two broad flavors—inline TVFs and multi-statement TVFs. Inline TVFs behave much like ITVFs, returning a table defined by a single SELECT. Multi-statement TVFs can execute multiple statements to build a result set, but they can be more complex to optimize and may hide performance costs behind a single function call. Choose TVFs when you want to encapsulate a complex data construction that would otherwise require multiple query blocks, but always be mindful of how the final plan is optimized by the database engine.

Two micro-cases to illustrate the choices

Micro-case C: DiscountPriceScalar

Goal: compute a discounted price for a given amount and discount rate.

What you do: implement a scalar function that takes @Price and @DiscountRate and returns @DiscountedPrice. Call it from a query that lists items with their discounted prices.

Rationale: demonstrates how a simple calculation can be packaged as a function, but also warns about potential per-row overhead if used in large result sets.

Micro-case D: ActiveProductsITVF

Goal: expose a filtered view of products that are currently active, with fields like ProductId, Name, Price, and AvailabilityDate.

What you do: implement an inline TVF that accepts @AsOfDate and returns a small, fixed schema. The function maps straightforward business rules to a clean SELECT, enabling callers to join or filter on the function's results efficiently.

Rationale: shows how an ITVF can improve readability and reusability without sacrificing performance.

Performance-minded guidelines

- Favor inline TVFs over scalar functions for complex data shaping that feeds into larger queries.

- Use scalar and ITTVFs when their use is clearly beneficial to readability or when the function's return type is a single value or a crisp, repeatable result.

- Avoid side effects inside functions; functions should be deterministic when possible, especially in production reporting or analytics workloads.

- Always test function usage in representative workloads to verify that the plan chosen by the optimizer remains efficient.

3) Trigger types, safe usage patterns and avoiding unintended side effects

Triggers are powerful, but they can also surprise you if you overuse them or implement them without safeguards.

DML triggers: most common triggers respond to data modifications (INSERT, UPDATE, DELETE). They can enforce business rules, keep audit trails, or maintain derived values. However, because they execute automatically, they can make debugging harder and can slow down the primary data-modification path if not carefully designed.

AFTER vs INSTEAD OF:

- AFTER triggers run after the triggering action completes. They're suited for auditing, cascading changes, or recalculating derived values when the source data has already changed.

- INSTEAD OF triggers intercept the operation and provide an alternative path. They're useful on views or when a modification requires complex logic not easily expressed in a single DML statement.

Safe usage patterns

- Keep triggers lightweight. Do minimal work inside a trigger; move heavy processing to asynchronous tasks or separate procedures when possible.

- Avoid deep nesting and infinite loops. Ensure triggers cannot cause recursive calls that lead to runaway execution.

- Use clear boundary lines. Triggers should not perform unrelated business logic or depend on external systems that could fail or slow down the main transaction.

- Provide a clean rollback path. If a trigger detects an error, make sure the entire transaction can roll back to preserve data integrity.

- Document trigger behavior. Note when and why a trigger fires, what it changes, and what data it relies on.

Two micro-cases help illustrate safe patterns

Micro-case E: AuditTrailTrigger

Goal: record, in an audit table, every INSERT into a transactions table.

What you do: implement an AFTER INSERT trigger on the transactions table that writes a compact audit row including the user, timestamp, and a snapshot of the inserted values. Ensure the trigger does not modify the inserted data in ways that could cause failures or recursion.

Rationale: demonstrates a common, relatively safe use of triggers—recording history without altering core business logic.

Micro-case F: ViewUpdateViaInsteadOfTrigger

Goal: allow complex updates to a denormalized view while keeping the base tables consistent.

What you do: create an INSTEAD OF UPDATE trigger on a view that translates the requested update into the appropriate changes on the underlying base tables. Keep the trigger's logic straightforward and avoid side effects beyond the necessary transformations.

Rationale: shows how triggers can enable convenient interfaces without breaking the rules of the base schema.

Exercises to practice

1) Create a modular stored procedure skeleton that accepts a few inputs and returns a simple output. Define the contract, add basic input validation, and implement a small core action. Time this in 20–30 minutes and verify the outputs with a couple of test calls.

2) Write a scalar function for a simple calculation (for example, tax on a price) and test it on several inputs. Compare performance when calling it from a query that returns thousands of rows versus calling it in isolation.

3) Implement an inline table-valued function that returns a filtered set of rows from a small table.

Validate that the function's output matches a hand-written equivalent query for a few date ranges or category filters.

4) Build a safe AFTER trigger that logs changes on a tiny table. Test by inserting, updating, and deleting a few rows and confirm the audit entries appear correctly without impacting the main operation's success. If possible, simulate a failure inside the trigger and verify the parent operation rolls back.

Templates and quick references

- Procedure contract template: Purpose, Parameters (names, types, IN/OUT), Returns,

Validation rules, Error signaling, Side effects, Testing notes.

- Function skeletons: Scalar function signature, Inline TVF signature, Multi-statement TVF outline, and guidance on appropriate use cases.

- Trigger skeleton: Trigger type (AFTER/INSTEAD OF), Target table/view, Key actions, Guardrails (recursion checks, error handling), and auditing notes.

Key Takeaway: Strong, well-documented contracts for procedures, carefully chosen function types for performance, and safe triggers keep your SQL predictable and maintainable.

Coming up next: Security, Auditing and Defensive SQL

1) Role-based access control, privilege management and row-level security models

2) Preventing SQL injection, input validation and secure parameterization

3) Auditing, data masking and encryption for compliance and privacy

Chapter 9

Security, Auditing and Defensive SQL

You will learn how to protect databases with smart access controls, guard against injection, and audit and mask data for privacy.

1) Role-based access control, privilege management and row-level security models

You start by framing who needs access to what data and why. Role-based access control (RBAC) is a simple way to group users by job function and assign a set of permissions to each group. The goal is to grant the minimum rights needed to get work done, never more. In practice, you define roles such as administrator, data_analyst, customer_service, and auditor. Each role receives a carefully chosen bundle of privileges: read access to certain tables, write permissions to specific columns, or the ability to run certain procedures. The key idea is least privilege: people should be able to do their jobs but nothing more. When you add up all the tasks each role must perform, you shape a clean, auditable map of who can do what.

Beyond roles, you manage privileges at a finer level. You separate duties so no single person has end-to-end control over critical data. For example, data_analysts can run reports and export aggregated data, but they cannot delete rows or change core table definitions. Administrators can alter the schema and manage users, but their access to sensitive customer data can be limited or reviewed. Privileges should be granted through a formal process and updated as roles evolve. Regular reviews catch drift—when someone changes jobs or when a project finishes, you adjust permissions so they stay aligned with current needs.

Row-level security (RLS) gives you another layer of protection. If your database supports RLS, you can enforce policies that limit which rows a user can see or alter. Think of a sales table that contains orders from many regions. With RLS, a user assigned to "regional_sales" can only view rows where region = their own. Or a technician who can access only the records they worked on. RLS policies work alongside RBAC to ensure data visibility follows the job's real requirements, not just the user's claimed role. You implement this by turning on RLS on the tables that hold sensitive data and then crafting policies that reference the user's identity, role, or other context. The result is a layered defense: even if a user somehow bypasses one gate, the data slice they see remains tightly scoped.

Two practical micro-cases help illustrate the idea. Case one involves a small customer-support team and a data_analyst group. The support team gets access to a customer contact table for service requests but not to the full financial records. The analyst can run broad reports, but you limit their access to read-only across the core tables and disable any ability to modify data unless they are explicitly granted by a supervisor. Case two shows a scenario with RLS. A retailer stores sales data in a single table. Each salesperson should see only their own customers' orders. You enable RLS on the table and write a policy that binds visibility to the user's identity or assigned region. The result is that even if a query tries to pull more data, the policy filters the rows, keeping sensitive information out of reach.

As you implement RBAC and RLS, you also build in oversight. Establish a process for periodic permission reviews, ideally quarterly or when teams shift. Have a documented approval trail for any change in access levels. Use logs to verify that permissions align with activity—the records can reveal mismatches, such as a user with broad read access who rarely uses it, or an account that has both read and write rights when only read is justified. In short, design for clarity, traceability, and adjustable controls. If a problem appears, you should be able to pinpoint who granted it, who uses it, and how to revoke it quickly.

A few practical cautions keep you on course. Don't rush to grant elevated access for temporary projects; instead, create a temporary role or run elevated tasks through controlled procedures that require approval and time-bound access. Be mindful of cross-role permissions that quietly compound, producing more access than intended. Finally, keep your policy language readable—security is strongest when the people enforcing it understand the rules and can explain them.

2) Preventing SQL injection, input validation and secure parameterization

The core problem is simple: attackers will try to slip bad data into your queries to alter behavior or steal information. Your defense is a three-pronged approach: lock down inputs, separate data from code, and use safe querying techniques. Start with input validation. Treat every piece of user-provided data as potentially dangerous. Wherever possible, enforce strict rules about what values are allowed. For example, if a field should only contain a 10-digit account number, reject anything else. When you validate inputs, you reduce the chance that harmful strings will reach your database.

Next, use secure parameterization for every query. Parameterized queries keep data separate from SQL code, so the database never treats user input as part of the command. This means you bind values to placeholders rather than concatenating strings to form SQL. The placeholders might be question marks or named parameters, depending on the system you use. By binding the values as the correct data types—strings, numbers, dates—you prevent tricky tricks that could change the query's intent. In practice, this is the fastest and most reliable line of defense against SQL injection.

A third line of defense is to restrict dynamic SQL. If you must build SQL strings at runtime, do it with extreme caution. Prefer fixed templates and strict binding whenever you can. When dynamic SQL is unavoidable, ensure you only allow a tightly controlled set of identifiers and values, and validate them against a known safe list before appending them to the final statement. Also, avoid exposing database construction code in web interfaces or APIs that could be manipulated by users. Keep the surface area small and well-checked.

Two micro-cases illustrate the difference. Case one shows a legacy pattern: building a query by string concatenation with user input for a search feature. If someone enters a special string like a SQL fragment, it can alter the query's behavior. The risk grows when the code uses multiple concatenated pieces to assemble a long statement. Case two shows best practice: a parameterized search that binds user input to a placeholder in the query, using a typed parameter. Even if the user provides a tricky value, the database treats it as data, not as part of the command. A good test is to try to inject an additional clause into the query; with parameterization, the harmful attempt fails because the input is never interpreted as code.

A practical tip you can apply today is to audit your codebase for any direct string assembly of queries. If you find it, rewrite those paths to use parameterized interfaces or prepared statements. Establish a default rule: no exception to parameterization, except for well-justified cases with formal risk assessments and approvals. And whenever you add new SQL, always review it for potential injection risks—this review becomes part of your standard code checks.

In addition to parameterization, you can harden input handling at the application edge. Sanitize inputs by trimming whitespace, normalizing case where it matters, and rejecting data with unusual lengths or formats. Where possible, implement allowlists of accepted values rather than relying on broad error handling to catch bad data. This reduces the chance that unexpected input travels to the database and causes trouble.

3) Auditing, data masking and encryption for compliance and privacy

Auditing and data protection go hand in hand. Auditing creates an evidence trail of who accessed what and when, which is essential for accountability and incident response. At a minimum, log successful and failed access attempts, changes to sensitive data, and administrative actions. The logs should be tamper-resistant or protected so that they remain trustworthy in the event of a security review. Use a centralized logging framework so you can search, filter, and analyze events across systems. Define a retention policy that keeps logs long enough to investigate incidents and to meet compliance needs, but not so long that you expose unnecessary data.

Masking is your friend when you need to show data to users who don't need the full details. Dynamic data masking can redact or partially reveal sensitive fields in query results, while still allowing legitimate users to perform their work. For example, you might display only the last four digits of a customer's phone number to a customer service representative, while the full number remains accessible to agents with higher privileges. Masking reduces risk without requiring a separate environment or dataset.

Encryption protects data at rest and in transit. Encrypt sensitive columns or entire databases so that a compromised file or backup cannot be read without the proper keys. Encryption in transit protects data as it moves between the client and server. It's also important to manage encryption keys carefully: use separate, access-controlled key stores, rotate keys on a regular schedule, and limit who can decrypt sensitive data. Even with strong encryption, you should minimize where and how long encrypted data is exposed to users and processes that do not need it.

In practice, these controls work together. An auditing system logs who accessed a masked field and when, while the masking ensures that the log entries still support incident investigation without exposing raw PII to every reader. A team of reviewers checks both the audit trails and the masking rules to ensure they align with privacy policies and regulatory expectations. You should also consider clear escalation paths if an audit uncovers unusual access patterns, and you should practice regular privacy reviews to keep up with changing standards and business needs.

Two micro-cases help ground these ideas. Case one: your system logs every access to a customer table and stores the events in an audit table. You also mask sensitive columns in the normal user interfaces, so analysts see only aggregated data unless they have higher clearance. Case two: you implement encryption for the most sensitive fields, with keys stored in a separate, tightly controlled service. Only when a user with the proper authority authenticates and is granted the right role can they decrypt and view the data. In both cases, you maintain accountability while protecting privacy.

Key Takeaway: Guard data with layered protections—start with solid access controls, defend against injections with safe querying and input checks, and protect privacy through auditing, masking, and encryption so data remains useful and safe.

Coming up next Subtittle: Real-World Patterns, Migration and Monitoring

1) Common patterns: slowly changing dimensions, star schema access and ETL queries,

2) Refactoring legacy SQL, migrating between DBMS and adapting to cloud services,

3) Benchmarking, query monitoring and operational practices for production systems

Chapter 10

Real-World Patterns, Migration and Monitoring

By the end of this chapter you will recognize common real-world SQL patterns, plan effective migrations between DBMS or to the cloud, and set up practical benchmarking and monitoring for production workloads.

Common patterns: Slowly Changing Dimensions, Star Schema Access, and ETL Queries

In real projects, data changes over time and you need your databases to reflect those changes without losing history. Slowly Changing Dimensions, or SCDs, are a family of methods that let you preserve past values while still showing current information. The simplest idea is to treat old data as a fixed record and add new records when something changes. The more common approach is to keep a history by adding time markers—begin and end dates, or a current flag—so you can reconstruct the state of your data at any moment. You may see different types of SCDs used in the same system, depending on what you're trying to track. Type 1 overwrites old values, Type 2 creates a new row for each change, and Type 3 keeps limited history in adjacent columns. In practice, you choose the method based on how long you need to keep the history and how you plan to query it. The key idea is to balance data accuracy with performance and storage costs.

Star schema access is another real-world pattern you'll encounter often. In this design, you have fact tables that record measurements or events and dimension tables that describe the who, what, where, and when behind those facts. This arrangement makes queries like "how did sales perform by region in the last quarter?" straightforward, because you join facts to dimensions and aggregate across the dimensions you care about. Access patterns tend to favor clear joins, well-defined grain, and carefully maintained foreign keys so the database can quickly locate the right records. The practical benefit is speed and simplicity for reports and dashboards, even when the underlying data is large.

ETL queries tie everything together. ETL stands for extract, transform, and load. In a real system, you'll pull data from multiple sources, tidy it up, and place it into a destination schema designed for reporting and analysis. A common pattern is to stage data first, apply transformations in a controlled sequence, and then load the clean data into your final tables. Incremental loads are favored when the source data changes gradually; you detect new or updated rows, transform them consistently, and upsert into the target. The challenge is to keep the staging area synchronized and to ensure that late-arriving data doesn't create gaps or duplicates in your reports. The practical upshot is reliable, repeatable data pipelines that you can monitor and adjust over time.

Micro-case 1: A customer history with SCD Type 2

You work on a customer table where you need to preserve every address a customer has ever used. When a customer moves, you don't overwrite the old address. Instead, you insert a new row with the new address and a new surrogate key, while you mark the previous row as no longer current. Your query for “the customer’s current address” looks for the row with the current flag set or the row whose end date is open. When your analytics needs a historical view, you can query across all rows to see the full travel of a customer over time. This approach keeps history intact and supports both detailed history analysis and current-state lookups.

Micro-case 2: Incremental ETL into a star schema

Your data warehouse uses a star schema with a central fact table and surrounding dimension tables. An ETL job runs in small, repeatable steps: extract new and changed data from sources, transform it to match the warehouse’s schema, and load it into staging tables. From there, you upsert dimension records, ensuring that slow-changing dimensions stay synchronized, and you populate fact records with the correct foreign keys. The key is to process only what has changed since the last run, keep the grain consistent, and verify that the resulting star schema can be queried efficiently by the reporting layer.

Refactoring legacy SQL, migrating between DBMS, and adapting to cloud services

Legacy SQL can be hard to read and hard to maintain because it often uses era-specific features, nested subqueries, or brittle assumptions about the database engine. Your job is to make it safer and clearer without changing the results. Start with readability: replace deeply nested blocks with modular pieces, and bring repeated patterns into common table expressions or views so the same logic is reused rather than copied. This reduces future maintenance and makes testing easier. Where nonstandard features creep in, aim for standard SQL patterns that work across systems, or document the differences clearly so future engineers can adapt quickly.

Migration between DBMS and cloud adaptation involves two main threads: compatibility and performance. Compatibility means checking data types, functions, and syntax that differ between systems. Some engines have unique functions or operators; you can usually replace them with standard SQL equivalents or with simple wrapper logic. Performance considerations include query plans, indexing strategies, and storage choices. In a migration, you want to preserve results, avoid changing business logic unintentionally, and keep load times reasonable while you validate behavior in the new environment. The general approach is to migrate incrementally, verify accuracy at each stage, and adjust your queries to fit the new engine's strengths and limits.

Micro-case 1: Refactoring a legacy analytic query

Imagine you have a large analytic query built with many nested subqueries. You rework it into a sequence of smaller, named components using common table expressions. Each piece performs a single transformation, and you join the pieces at the end. This makes the intent clearer and helps you test each step separately. After refactoring, you compare results with the old version to confirm equivalence, then you profile the new query to confirm it runs at least as fast as the original or better with the same data.

Micro-case 2: Migrating from an on-premises DBMS to a cloud service

In a migration, you start by mapping core data types and ensuring data integrity is preserved. You validate critical queries in the new environment and adjust for any differences in function behavior or indexing options. You also consider how you'll scale storage and compute in the cloud, choosing approaches that support your typical workloads—reporting, analytics, or mixed transactions. The goal is to maintain correct results while taking advantage of the cloud's flexibility and resilience, without introducing unnecessary complexity or cost.

Benchmarking, query monitoring, and operational practices for production systems

At production scale, you must measure, track, and respond to how your queries perform under real workloads. Benchmarking gives you a baseline so you can tell when a change actually improves or degrades performance. Start with a representative workload that mirrors the patterns you see in reports and dashboards. Run the workload under controlled conditions and record key metrics such as latency, throughput, and resource usage. Baselines let you distinguish normal variation from real regressions.

Monitoring turns numbers into action. You set up dashboards or simple reports that show top resource users, failed jobs, and long-running queries. Alerts trigger when performance crosses a threshold, so you can investigate before users notice a slowdown. A good monitoring practice includes tracing the execution time of critical queries, looking at execution plans when something slows down, and keeping an eye on backlog or queue lengths in ETL processes. This visibility helps you tune systems proactively rather than reactively.

Operational practices include repeatable deployment, regression checks, and runbooks. You want predictable changes, so you test every modification against the same data set and expected results. You maintain runbooks that describe how to recover from common problems, restore data, or roll back deployments if needed. Documentation and automation go a long way toward reliability.

Two practical micro-cases demonstrate these ideas. In the first, you baseline a nightly ETL job that loads a week of data. You record its duration, the amount of data processed, and the success rate. After optimizing a few steps—such as simplifying joins or pruning unnecessary calculations—you re-run the baseline and compare results. If the run time drops meaningfully and accuracy is preserved, you've improved the pipeline. In the second, you implement a simple monitoring dashboard that lists the top five slowest queries from the past 24 hours, flags any query that exceeds a normal range, and shows a trend line of total daily throughput. This gives you quick visibility into how your production system behaves and where to focus effort.

Tools, templates, and practical templates you can copy

Migration readiness checklist:

1. Map data types and verify basic data integrity between the old and new environments.

2. Identify nonstandard features or vendor-specific functions and plan standard equivalents.

3. Prepare a small, representative test dataset and reproduce critical queries in the new engine.

4. Validate results against the original environment for several typical workloads.

5. Develop a staged migration plan with a clear rollback option.

Baseline and monitoring templates:

1. Baseline workload description: list representative queries, data volumes, and typical runtimes.

2. Monitoring dashboard sketch: include top slowest queries, average latency, and error counts.

3. Query plan review sheet: capture explain plans, estimated vs. actual costs, and any index recommendations.

4. Runbook outline: steps for common issues, from failed ETL runs to degraded query performance.

Troubleshooting quick fixes you can apply

If a query slows down after migration, check for:

1) Missing or ineffective indexes in the new environment.

2) Differences in data types that degrade performance or accuracy.

3) Changes in execution plans due to optimizer behavior.

4) Nonstandard functions being used in the query that don't map cleanly to the new engine.

If an ETL job lags, consider:

1) Breaking large transformations into smaller, testable steps.

2) Running heavy steps in parallel if the platform allows it.

3) Reducing data movement by staging more data locally within the environment.

4) Verifying data freshness and late-arriving data handling rules.

Key Takeaway: Real-world SQL work blends preserving history, organizing data for fast access, and keeping pipelines reliable through careful migration and clear monitoring.

Transition: In the next chapter, you'll dive deeper into mastering the actual techniques that power these patterns—how to design robust data models, implement reliable ETL pipelines, and validate results with reproducible tests. You'll practice turning theory into repeatable, production-ready workflows that still leave room for experimentation and improvement.

Dear Reader,

Thank you for exploring this series focused on failures and the power of comeback stories. If you find value in these stories and believe in the importance of embracing setbacks as part of growth, we appreciate your support. Please consider sharing a positive review on the platform where you accessed this series.

Your feedback helps spread the message, inspiring more young readers to see challenges as opportunities and to believe in their potential. We understand that mistakes happen, and we thank you for your understanding.